This library edition published in 2015 by Walter Foster Publishing,
a division of Quarto Publishing Group USA Inc.
3 Wrigley, Suite A
Irvine, CA 92618

Distributed in the United States and Canada by
Lerner Publisher Services
241 First Avenue North
Minneapolis, MN 55401 U.S.A.
www.lernerbooks.com

First Library Edition

012015
18582

9 8 7 6 5 4 3 2 1

Animals

From playful kittens to fluffy bunnies, drawing baby animals is a wonderful, fun, and rewarding challenge. Besides being too cute for words, baby animals require a softer drawing technique than their adult counterparts do. And graphite pencil is the perfect medium for capturing their youthful likenesses. In this book, you'll learn tricks and techniques to creating the characteristics (such as soft fur, downy feathers, and large, expressive eyes) that will make your baby animal drawings look amazingly realistic. You'll also find in-depth information on tools and materials and shading techniques, as well as 12 simple, step-by-step projects that include a lion cub, a giraffe calf, and a Doberman puppy. I hope this book gives you the information and inspiration you need to start drawing your own adorable baby animals.

—Cindy Smith

CONTENTS

Tools & Materials

Drawing is not only fun, but it also is an important art form in itself. Even when you write or print your name, you are actually drawing! If you organize the lines, you can make shapes; and when you carry that a bit further and add dark and light shading, your drawings begin to take on a three-dimensional form and look more realistic. One of the great things about drawing is that you can do it anywhere, and the materials are very inexpensive. You do get what you pay for, though, so purchase the best you can afford at the time, and upgrade your supplies whenever possible. Although anything that will make a mark can be used for some type of drawing, you'll want to make certain your magnificent efforts will last and not fade over time. Here are some materials that will get you off to a good start.

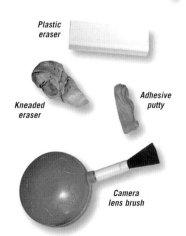

▶ **Sketch Pads** You can buy spiral-bound, stitched, or gum-bound sketchbooks in a variety of sizes. The paper in most sketchbooks is not designed for finished works—sketching is a form of visual note taking, and you should not worry about producing masterpieces with them. You may want to carry a small notebook-sized sketchbook with you so you can sketch whenever the mood strikes. It's a good idea to carry a larger sketchbook when drawing on location.

▲ **Work Station** You don't need a professional drafting table to start drawing—many brilliant drawings have been created on a kitchen table! You'll need a hard surface to use as a drawing board (or purchase a drawing board from an art supply store), and something to prop up the board with, such as a brick or a stack of books. Good lighting is essential—it's best to work in natural light, but you also can purchase a daylight bulb, which gives off a good white light and eliminates the yellow glare of standard bulbs. Make sure the lighting is direct and that there are no shadows falling across your work area. Also, you'll want to have a comfortable chair that supports your back.

▶ **Paper** Drawing paper is available in a range of surface textures: smooth grain (*plate finish* and *hot pressed*), medium grain (*cold pressed*), and rough to very rough. Rough paper is ideal when using charcoal, whereas smooth paper is best for watercolor washes. The heavier the weight of the paper, the thicker it is. Thicker papers are better for graphite drawings because they can withstand erasing far better than thinner papers can. Be sure to purchase acid-free paper, as acid causes paper to turn yellow over time.

▶ **Blending Tools** Paper stumps (also called "tortillons") are used to blend or smudge areas of graphite into a flat, even tone. Be careful when using blending tools, as they tend to push the graphite into the paper, making the area difficult to erase. Another good way to blend is to wrap a chamois cloth around your finger. Never use your finger alone for blending—your skin contains oils that could damage the paper.

◀ **Sharpeners** Clutch pencils (see page 3) require special sharpeners, which you can find at art and craft stores. A regular handheld sharpener can be used for wood-cased and woodless pencils, but be sure to have several sharpeners on hand as these pencils can become dull. You can also purchase an electric sharpener, but it affords less control over the shape of the pencil tip.

Plastic eraser

Kneaded eraser

Adhesive putty

Camera lens brush

◀ **Erasers** Mistakes are inevitable, so it's good to have a few erasers on hand. Plastic art erasers are good for removing harder pencil marks and for erasing large areas. Be careful when using this type of eraser, as rubbing too hard will damage the surface of the paper. This eraser also leaves crumbs, so be sure to softly brush them away with a makeup or camera lens brush. Kneaded erasers are very pliable; you can mold them into different shapes. Instead of rubbing the kneaded eraser across the paper, gently dab at the area to remove or lighten tone. Another great tool is adhesive putty, made for tacking posters to a wall. Like a kneaded eraser, it can be molded and won't damage the paper.

PENCILS

Soft pencils (labeled "B") produce strong, black tones; hard pencils (labeled "H") create lighter marks. The higher the number that accompanies the letter, the harder or softer the lead. (For example, a 4B pencil is softer than a 2B pencil.) HB and F pencils are used for middle grades. We recommend starting with the following range of wood-cased pencils: 2H, H, HB, F, B, and 2B. As your skills develop, you can experiment with different types of pencils. Some artists like to use clutch pencils (also called "mechanical pencils"), which require special sharpeners (see page 2). You can also purchase woodless graphite pencils, which are great for covering large areas with tone or for making quick sketches. These pencils are usually very soft, and the graphite breaks easily. Charcoal pencils are also good for making very dark black marks. Keep in mind that tones vary among manufacturers—one brand's HB may look very different from another brand's, so try to stick with one brand of pencil for a consistent range of tones.

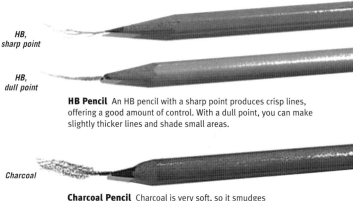

HB, sharp point

HB, dull point

HB Pencil An HB pencil with a sharp point produces crisp lines, offering a good amount of control. With a dull point, you can make slightly thicker lines and shade small areas.

Charcoal

Charcoal Pencil Charcoal is very soft, so it smudges easily and makes a dark mark.

Clutch pencil

Clutch Pencil A clutch pencil doesn't change in weight or length, so you never need to adjust your feel for it.

Woodless pencil

Woodless Pencil A woodless pencil is a solid core of graphite covered with a thin sheath of plastic. It is great for creating broad areas of tone.

◄ **Spray Fix** A fixative "sets" a drawing and protects it from smearing. Some artists avoid using fixative on pencil drawings because it tends to deepen the light shadings and eliminate some delicate values. However, fixative works well for charcoal drawings. Fixative is available in spray cans or in bottles, but you need a mouth atomizer to use bottled fixative. Spray cans are more convenient, and they give a finer spray and more even coverage.

TRACING AND TRANSFERRING

Place a sheet of tracing paper on top of your photo reference and trace the major outlines of the animal. Then use transfer paper—thin sheets of paper that are coated on one side with an even application of graphite—to transfer the image to your drawing paper. Place the transfer paper on top of your drawing paper, graphite-side down, holding the transfer paper in place with artist's tape. Then place the tracing paper on top of the transfer paper (you may need to enlarge or reduce the image on a photocopier to fit your drawing paper) and lightly trace the lines with a pencil or a sharp object that won't leave a mark, such as a stylus or the pointed edge of the handle of a thin paintbrush. The lines will transfer to the drawing paper below.

You can purchase transfer paper at an art supply store, or you can make your own. Just cover the back of the traced image with an even layer of graphite, place the graphite side on top of the drawing paper, and lightly trace the lines of the sketch to transfer them. Check underneath the transfer paper occasionally to make sure the lines that have transferred aren't too light or too dark.

THE ELEMENTS OF DRAWING

Drawing consists of three elements: line, shape, and form. The shape of an object can be described with simple one-dimensional line. The three-dimensional version of the shape is known as the object's "form." In pencil drawing, variations in value (the relative lightness or darkness of black or a color) describe form, giving an object the illusion of depth. In pencil drawing, values range from black (the darkest value) through different shades of gray to white (the lightest value). To make a two-dimensional object appear three-dimensional, you must pay attention to the values of the highlights and shadows. When shading a subject, you must always consider the light source, as this is what determines where your highlights and shadows will be.

MOVING FROM SHAPE TO FORM

The first step in creating an object is establishing a line drawing or outline to delineate the flat area that the object takes up. This is known as the "shape" of the object. The four basic shapes—the rectangle, circle, triangle, and square—can appear to be three-dimensional by adding a few carefully placed lines that suggest additional planes. By adding ellipses to the rectangle, circle, and triangle, you've given the shapes dimension and have begun to produce a form within space. Now the shapes are a cylinder, sphere, and cone. Add a second square above and to the side of the first square, connect them with parallel lines, and you have a cube.

ADDING VALUE TO CREATE FORM

A shape can be further defined by showing how light hits the object to create highlights and shadows. First note from which direction the source of light is coming. (In these examples, the light source is beaming from the upper right.) Then add the shadows accordingly, as shown in the examples below. The *core shadow* is the darkest area on the object and is opposite the light source. The *cast shadow* is what is thrown onto a nearby surface by the object. The *highlight* is the lightest area on the object, where the reflection of light is strongest. *Reflected light,* often overlooked by beginners, is surrounding light reflected into the shadowed area of an object.

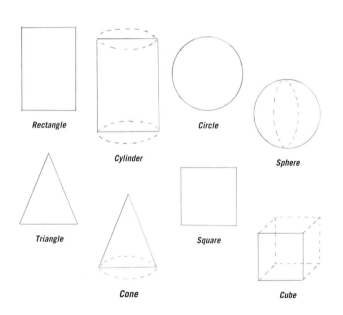

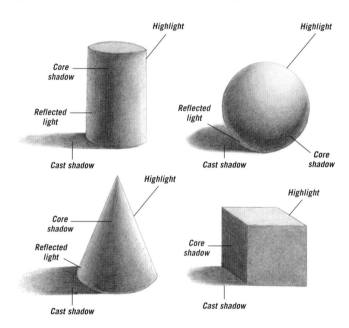

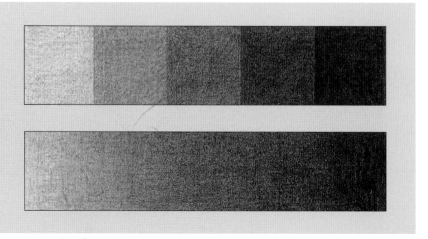

CREATING VALUE SCALES

Just as a musician uses a musical scale to measure a range of notes, an artist uses a value scale to measure changes in value. You can refer to the value scale so you'll always know how dark to make your dark values and how light to make your highlights. The scale also serves as a guide for transitioning from lighter to darker shades. Making your own value scale will help familiarize you with the different variations in value. Work from light to dark, adding more and more tone for successively darker values (as shown at upper right). Then create a blended value scale (shown at lower right). Use a tortillon to smudge and blend each value into its neighboring value from light to dark to create a gradation.

BASIC PENCIL TECHNIQUES

You can create an incredible variety of effects with a pencil. By using various hand positions and shading techniques, you can produce a world of different lines and strokes. If you vary the way you hold the pencil, the mark the pencil makes changes. It's just as important to notice your pencil point. The point is every bit as essential as the type of lead in the pencil. Experiment with different hand positions and techniques to see what your pencil can do!

GRIPPING THE PENCIL

Many artists use two main hand positions for drawing. The writing position is good for very detailed work that requires fine hand control. The underhand position allows for a freer stroke with more arm movement—the motion is almost like painting. (See the captions below for more information on using both hand positions.)

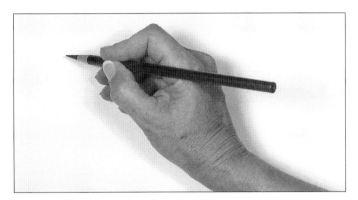

Using the Writing Position This familiar position provides the most control. The accurate, precise lines that result are perfect for rendering fine details and accents. When your hand is in this position, place a clean sheet of paper under your hand to prevent smudging.

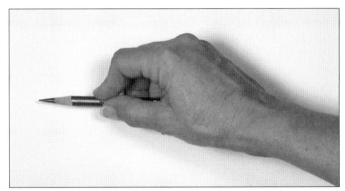

Using the Underhand Position Pick up the pencil with your hand over it, holding the pencil between the thumb and index finger; the remaining fingers can rest alongside the pencil. You can create beautiful shading effects from this position.

PRACTICING BASIC TECHNIQUES

By studying the basic pencil techniques below, you can learn to render everything from the rough, wrinkled skin of an elephant to the soft, fluffy fur of a bunny. Whatever techniques you use, though, remember to shade evenly. Shading in a mechanical, side-to-side direction, with each stroke ending below the last, can create unwanted bands of tone throughout the shaded area. Instead try shading evenly, in a back-and-forth motion over the same area, varying the spot where the pencil point changes direction.

Hatching This basic method of shading involves filling an area with a series of parallel strokes. The closer the strokes, the darker the tone will be.

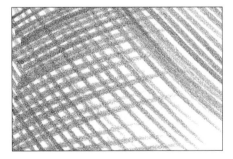

Crosshatching For darker shading, place layers of parallel strokes on top of one another at varying angles. Again, make darker values by placing the strokes closer together.

Gradating To create gradated values (from dark to light), apply heavy pressure with the side of your pencil, gradually lightening the pressure as you stroke.

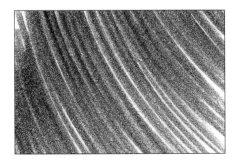

Shading Darkly By applying heavy pressure to the pencil, you can create dark, linear areas of shading.

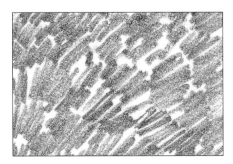

Shading with Texture For a mottled texture, use the side of the pencil tip to apply small, uneven strokes.

Blending To smooth out the transitions between strokes, gently rub the lines with a tortillon or tissue.

5

OTHER WAYS TO SHADE

PRACTICING LINES

When drawing lines, it is not necessary to always use a sharp point. In fact, sometimes a blunt point may create a more desirable effect. When using larger lead diameters, the effect of a blunt point is even more evident. Play around with your pencils to familiarize yourself with the different types of lines they can create. Make every kind of stroke you can think of, using both a sharp point and a blunt point. Practice the strokes below to help you loosen up.

As you experiment, you will find that some of your doodles will bring to mind certain imagery or textures. For example, little Vs can be reminiscent of birds flying, whereas wavy lines can indicate water.

"PAINTING" WITH PENCIL

When you use painterly strokes, your drawing will take on a new dimension. Think of your pencil as a brush and allow yourself to put more of your arm into the stroke. To create this effect, try using the underhand position, holding your pencil between your thumb and index finger and using the side of the pencil. (See page 5.) If you rotate the pencil in your hand every few strokes, you will not have to sharpen it as frequently. The larger the lead, the wider the stroke will be. The softer the lead, the more painterly an effect you will have. The examples below were all made on smooth paper with a 6B pencil, but you can experiment with rough papers for more broken effects.

Drawing with a Sharp Point First draw a series of parallel lines. Try them vertically; then angle them. Make some of them curved, trying both short and long strokes. Then try some wavy lines at an angle and some with short, vertical strokes. Try making a spiral and then grouping short, curved lines together. Then practice varying the weight of the line as you draw. Os, Vs, and Us are some of the most common alphabet shapes used in drawing.

▶ **Starting Simply** First experiment with vertical, horizontal, and curved strokes. Keep the strokes close together and begin with heavy pressure. Then lighten the pressure with each stroke.

▶ **Varying the Pressure** Randomly cover the area with tone, varying the pressure at different points. Continue to keep your strokes loose.

Drawing with a Blunt Point It is good to take the same exercises and try them with a blunt point. Even if you use the same hand positions and strokes, the results will be different when you switch pencils. Take a look at these examples. The same shapes were drawn with both pencils, but the blunt pencil produced different images. You can create a blunt point by rubbing the tip of the pencil on a sandpaper block or on a rough piece of paper.

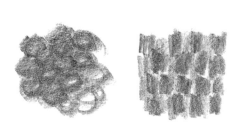

▶ **Using Smaller Strokes** Make small circles for the first example. This is reminiscent of leathery animal skin. For the second example (at far right), use short, alternating strokes of heavy and light pressure to create a pattern that is similar to stone or brick.

▶ **Loosening Up** Use long vertical strokes, varying the pressure for each stroke until you start to see long grass (near right). Now create short spiral movements with your arm (far right, above). Then use a wavy movement, varying the pressure (far right, below).

FINDING YOUR STYLE

Many great artists of the past can now be identified by their unique experiments with line. Van Gogh's drawings were a feast of calligraphic lines; Seurat became synonymous with pointillism; and Giacometti was famous for his scribble. Find your own style!

▶ **Using Criss-Crossed Strokes** If you like a good deal of fine detail in your work, you'll find that crosshatching allows you a lot of control (see page 5). You can adjust the depth of your shading by changing the distance between your strokes.

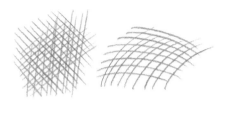

▶ **Sketching Circular Scribbles** If you work with round, loose strokes like these, you are probably very experimental with your art. These looping lines suggest a free-form style that is more concerned with evoking a mood than with creating precise details.

▶ **Drawing Small Dots** This technique is called "stippling"—many small dots are used to create a larger picture. Make the points different sizes to create various depths and shading effects. Stippling takes a great deal of precision and practice.

▶ **Simulating Brush-strokes** You can create the illusion of brushstrokes by using short, sweeping lines. This captures the feeling of painting but allows you the same control you would get from crosshatching. These strokes are ideal for a stylistic approach.

NEGATIVE DRAWING

Negative drawing means defining an object by filling in the area around it rather than the object itself. This method is particularly useful when the object in the foreground is lighter in tone than the background, as well as for drawing hair. You can easily draw hair using lines, but how do you draw light hair? You draw the negative shadows between the hairs.

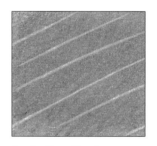

Using Negative Drawing for Hair Once the negative space is shaded (above left), you can add texture and tone to individual hairs to give them more realism and depth (above right).

DRAWING WITH ERASERS

Graphite is very easy to manipulate with erasers. Not only can you correct mistakes, but you can use them to soften lines, create lighter shading, pull out highlights, and even draw. You can also use erasers to lighten objects, suggesting distance. The process of creating light areas or shapes on a darker graphite background is called "lifting out."

Drawing Lines with an Eraser Quickly stroking the edge of a hard eraser across graphite results in a clear line that can be used to suggest highlights.

Drawing Hair To create this hair texture, apply a solid layer of shading. Then use the tip of an eraser to pull out short lines in the direction of hair growth.

SMUDGING

Smudging is an important technique for creating shading and gradients. Use a tortillon or chamois cloth to blend your strokes. It is important to not use your finger, because your hand, even if clean, has natural oils that can damage your art.

◀ **Smudging on Rough Surfaces** Use a 6B pencil on rough paper. Make your strokes with the side of the pencil and blend. In this example, the effect is very granular.

◀ **Smudging on Smooth Surfaces** Use a 4B pencil on plate-finish paper. Stroke with the side of the pencil, and then blend your strokes with a tortillon.

BUNNY

Step One I begin by using an HB pencil to sketch the bunny freehand. The basic roundness of the bunny's head and body makes this an easy task. Then I indicate (or "map out") the areas of darkest fur.

Step Two Now I switch to a 2B pencil and start defining the eye (see "Shading the Eye" on page 9), nose, and ears. Then I use an H pencil to place the whisker markings and whiskers. I use the same pencil to begin laying down short strokes in the darkest areas of fur, as well as add the cast shadow under the bunny.

Step Three With a 4B pencil, I fill in the darkest areas of fur. I use quick, short, tapering strokes, careful to leave openings for the lighter and midtone areas of fur. I concentrate on drawing in the direction of fur growth, and I apply longer strokes for the hair around the belly. Using a large bristle brush (sometimes called a "gesso brush"), I blend the soft 4B strokes to create a soft midtone. Then I darken the whiskers, using a 2H pencil for the lighter whiskers and an H for the darker ones.

Step Four Next I fill in the midtone areas of fur on the head and body using 2B and H pencils, occasionally blending the strokes with the bristle brush. For the darker area around the nose, I use an H pencil. Then I create various V shapes throughout the fur to achieve a "clumpy" look, and I begin adding some fur to the edges of the bunny's left ear.

▶ **Step Five** I continue applying the dark and midtone fur on the feet and ears, and I use a tortillon to blend the soft, fleshy area inside the ears. I return to the pencil and go over the entire bunny, defining shadows and shapes. Then I form my kneaded eraser into a point to "draw" the lightest hairs. I also use the kneaded eraser to lift out lighter shapes in the fur on the belly, chest, and around the eyes.

Step Six To create greater contrast, I accent all the dark and light areas in the fur. Then I add some plants and pebbles to "ground" the bunny. I build up the pebbles and sand with a 4B pencil and then use a tortillon to blend the tone. I shape a kneaded eraser into a point and use it to dab at the rocks to create highlights.

SHADING THE EYE

Step One First I use a 2B to darken the outlines of the eye and pupil. I am careful to avoid the highlight, which overlaps the iris for a more natural appearance.

Step Two I use a 2B to fill in the iris and blend it with a tortillon; I use a 4B to fill in the pupil. I also define the rim around the eye with a 2B and blend the tone with a tortillon.

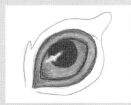

Step Three I use a 4B to soften the edges of the rim, leaving a lighter strip in the middle to give the rim a rounded look. I add a touch of light shading to each corner of the eye with a 4B. Then I add a layer of H to slightly darken the iris. I am careful to darken the iris more at the upper lid to set it back into the eyelid. Then I use my kneaded eraser to lighten the highlight. Finally, I use a 4B to make the pupil as dark as possible.

Step Four For the white areas around the rim, I use a 2B to add radiating lines; then I use the tortillon to blend them outward from the rim of the eye.

KITTEN

Step One I place a sheet of tracing paper on top of my reference photo and lightly trace the outline and facial features of the kitten, being careful to keep the outline light. I also outline the fur, following the direction of the hair growth. Once the outline has been established, I freehand the whiskers and the stripes in the fur.

Step Two I transfer the outline to my drawing paper (see "Tracing and Transferring" on page 3) and then begin defining the facial features, paying particular attention to the eyes, as they will be the focal point of this drawing. I reinforce the darkest areas of the face using a 2B pencil, but I am careful to leave a highlight in each eye. I want these highlights to be the lightest areas of the drawing, with the pupils being the darkest.

Step Three I continue shading the kitten, using a 2B pencil to emphasize the darkest areas of the fur with quick, short, tapering strokes that are lifted at the end. I create the whiskers by drawing around them (see "Negative Drawing" on page 7). Next I add tone to the eyes with an H pencil, leaving highlights in each. Then I use a tortillon to soften the irises.

Step Four I lay in the midtone areas of the fur with an H pencil and use a 2H pencil for the slightly lighter fur. Next I blend the dark areas and midtones together with the bristle brush, using a sweeping back-and-forth motion.

◄ Step Five I lift out highlights from the fur with a kneaded eraser pinched to a sharp edge. I also use the pinched edge of the eraser to lighten the whiskers. With an H pencil, I darken the areas at the base of the whiskers. Next I add some grass under the kitten using an H pencil so it does not appear to be floating in the air. Then I switch to a 2B pencil to fill in the areas between the grass blades, blending them with the bristle brush.

► Step Six I go over the darkest areas with a 4B pencil, and I lift out graphite with my kneaded eraser in the lightest areas for greater contrast. I make sure the highlight in each eye is as bright as it can be. Although I use an electric eraser for the brightest highlights, a kneaded eraser shaped into a point will also work. Finally, I add more detail to the grass, using an H pencil to define the blades. I am careful not to render too much detail in the grass, as the focus of this drawing should be the adorable kitten.

Cindy Smith

11

GOSLING

▶ **Step One** I start by placing a sheet of tracing paper over my reference photo and tracing the gosling. Then I freehand the water ripples and the rock. I am careful not to make a solid outline for the gosling. Instead, I use short, quick strokes to indicate its soft feathers. Next I transfer the outlines to a piece of drawing paper.

▶ **Step Two** With a 4B pencil, I outline the eye and fill in the pupil. Then I use a 2B to fill in the iris and blend the tone with a tortillon. I use a 2B to establish the shadow areas on the gosling, following the direction of the feathers. Next I darken the area where the gosling's body meets the water. Then I begin refining the gosling's fluff with an extremely sharp 2B pencil. I use a 2B for the darkest areas and an H for the midtones. I apply the lighter areas last with a 2H. I use sharp, quick, tapering strokes overlapping each toned area, starting with the darkest areas. I sharpen my pencil every few strokes.

▶ **Step Three** I continue rendering the fluff on the gosling's head, working in the same fashion as on the body. I use an H pencil for the subtle shadows around the eyes and on the bill. Then I go over the entire gosling, emphasizing shadows and lifting out highlights with a kneaded eraser. Using a 4B, I begin placing the darkest darks in the water and blend these with a tortillon. I also indicate the darkest areas of the rock with the 4B. Then I lift out some soft feathers along the outline of the gosling with a kneaded eraser.

▶ **Step Four** Next I dip a tortillon in graphite powder (shavings I collect from sharpening all my pencils) and softly spread the powder (which is a combination of different grades of pencil) in the midtone areas of the water. I lift out highlights in the water using a kneaded eraser pinched to a sharp edge. Then I use a 4B to strengthen the darkest areas of the water and rock.

▶ **Step Five** I create the rock with the same techniques I used for the water: I use a 4B for the darkest areas, dip a tortillon in graphite powder for the midtones, and pull out highlights with a kneaded eraser.

Step Six After leaving the drawing alone for a few days, I come back to it with fresh eyes. I notice that the gosling blends in with the water, so I use an H pencil to darken lighter areas of the water and a 2B pencil for deeper areas. Then I lift out some tone from the gosling's chest to create greater contrast with the water. Now I can see the gosling more clearly. It is often beneficial to come back to a piece after a few days and make any necessary adjustments.

13

FOAL

Step One Using tracing paper, I outline the foal and its facial features, and then I freehand the identifying markings on the rest of its body. This helps me map out the light and dark values of the body. Next I transfer the outline to drawing paper.

Step Two With a 2B, I begin isolating the darkest areas, use varying degrees of pressure to give the drawing some depth. I concentrate on refining the initial outline and placing the eyes and other facial features.

Step Three Next I darken the eyes, nostrils, and ears with a 4B. I use a 2B for the muzzle and start the head and neck with the same pencil. I blend the muzzle with a tortillon to make it appear smooth. On the neck, I use short, quick, tapering strokes and blend with the bristle brush. I fill in the darker areas of the body and legs with a 4B. Using the "map" from step one as a guide, I follow the direction of hair growth. I vary my strokes for the different types of hair; some strokes are short and tapered, whereas some are more of a scribble.

Step Four I finish the head with a sharp 2B, using short strokes and blending with the bristle brush. Then I apply the midtone areas of the body and legs using a 2B. I continue varying the types and directions of my strokes, blocking in the patterns and hair types. Then I blend the tone with a tortillon.

▶ **Step Five** I begin refining the darks and lights in the hair patterns. I fill in the lighter areas of the hair with an H pencil and then go back over the same area with a 2B or 4B depending on the tone, creating a series of layers. In the lightest areas, I use my kneaded eraser to lift out the highlights. I pinch the eraser to a sharp edge and, with a flick here and there, lift out graphite for individual lighter hairs. For the tail and mane, I use a 2B to lay in the lighter hair and a 4B to create depth. Then I blend the tone with the bristle brush.

◀ **Step Six** Now I go over the entire horse, defining the light and dark areas and giving the hair its final depth and texture. Then I add a simple ground with a 4B, quickly indicating rocks and gravel and then blending with the bristle brush to spread the tone. Finally, I use a kneaded eraser to lift out subtle highlights. My goal for the ground is to make it simple and not detract from the foal.

Doberman puppy

Step One To begin this drawing, I place a sheet of tracing paper on top of my reference photo and lightly trace the outline and facial features of the puppy. I also map out the major value areas, such as the patches of light fur on the chest and paws, as well as the light eyebrows. Then I transfer the outline to drawing paper.

Step Two Starting with the eyes, I outline and darken the pupils with a 4B. Then I fill in the iris with a 2B, smoothing the tone with a tortillon to achieve a glossy look. I use the same 2B to begin creating the bumpy texture on the nose, being careful to leave the top and front of the nose lighter to help create the form. Then I use a 4B to darken the nostrils. (See "Drawing the Nose and Muzzle" on page 17 for more information.)

Step Three Using a 4B pencil, I add long, linear strokes to the darkest areas of the ears, face, paws, and body. As I draw, I make sure my lines follow the direction of the hair growth, noting where the hair swirls and changes direction (mostly on the chest and upper areas of the front legs). With a 2B pencil, I re-outline the claws, and I add small dots on the muzzle to indicate the whisker markings. To create the whiskers that hang down from the muzzle, I simply draw around these areas when shading the upper chest.

Step Four I continue to build up the darkest areas on the chest, shoulders, and face with the 4B pencil, placing more pressure on the pencil for darker areas and using less pressure for lighter areas. I avoid adding tone to the light areas I established in my initial sketch.

► Step Five Next I use a rounded 2B pencil and create the lighter tones in the areas I had previously avoided: the legs, paws, chest, muzzle, and eyebrows. I use the same pencil to further shade the upper part of the face, adding two or three layers of graphite for a darker tone. For areas in shadow, I blend the tone with a tortillon.

DRAWING THE NOSE AND MUZZLE

Step One I start by sketching the shape of the nose and muzzle, including the whiskers and the vertical crease through the middle of the nose. Then I use a 2B pencil to indicate the main areas of shadow.

Step Two I use a dull 2B to cover the nose with small circular strokes. Note that I shorten the vertical crease a bit at this stage.

Step Three I add another layer of circular strokes in the midtone areas. Then I switch to a 4B and add more circular strokes to the upper part of the nose, being careful not to create any solid areas of graphite. These harsh separations between light and dark give the nose a wet appearance. To add tone to the muzzle area, I use an H pencil and a light touch. Then I add small dots to indicate the whisker markings.

Step Four Now I make the dark areas even darker with the 4B pencil. I darken the upper area in the nostrils, leaving the outer edges lighter. Then I use small, tight circular strokes on the front of the nose and larger circular strokes on the dark strip above the nose. I lift out tone in areas with a kneaded eraser for highlights. I add more tone to the muzzle with the H pencil, and I further define the whiskers and whisker markings. Then I feather short strokes from the top of the nose up onto the bridge.

◄ Step Six Now I use a 4B to further darken the body, upper part of the face, ears, and upper part of the front legs. Where needed, such as along the edges of the front legs and shoulders, I lift out tone with a kneaded eraser to create highlights. Returning to the eyes, I make the pupils as dark as possible, lifting out a highlight in each when finished. I also add more tone to the top of the nose and nostrils. As a final touch, I use a 2H to shade lightly under the pup's chest and front legs, and I blend the tone with a tortillon.

BEAR CUB

▶ **Step One** I outline the basic shape and facial features of the cub using tracing paper. Then I free-hand sketch the tree and the identifying marks of the cub. Now I transfer the outlines to a piece of drawing paper.

▶ **Step Two** I begin the eyes by outlining them with a 4B. I use a 2B for the iris, being careful to leave highlights, and then I blend with a tortillon. I use an H pencil to identify the area around the eyes and a 4B pencil for the nostrils. Using circular strokes, I fill in the rest of the nose with a 2B. I use my 4B with short, tapering strokes on the ears, and I add the darkest areas on the paws, back leg, and parts of the tree. Then I use the bristle brush to blend the graphite.

▶ **Step Three** I continue working on the head with a 2B, using short, tapering strokes that follow the direction of hair growth. Then I take my 4B and go back over the head, adding darker strokes for depth. Next I blend the tones together with the bristle brush. I use a 2B and an H for the muzzle and lighter areas of the face. Then I use a 2B to start identifying the darker areas of the fur, such as under the arms, under the chin, on the back leg, and between the toes. For the longer, darker fur I use a 4B with tapering strokes; for the fuzzier fur (such as under the chin), I use a dull 4B and a scribbling motion.

▶ **Step Four** Now I use a very sharp 2B to lay in some midtones on the cub's body with short, tapering strokes. I spread the tone often with the bristle brush. Then I use a kneaded eraser to pull out tone for the lightest areas of fur.

▶ **Step Five** Next I go back and reinforce my previous work with a 2B pencil, adding more strokes for depth in the midtone areas. Then I use a 4B to define the darkest darks. I am careful to vary my strokes, as some areas of the cub's fur are wavy or matted rather than straight.

▶ **Step Six** I continue adding depth to the cub by filling in the darker areas with a 4B and using a 2B to fill in more of the midtone areas. I build up several layers to make the fur appear more dense. Now I start developing the tree by identifying the dark crevices with a 4B. I use my tortillon to spread and blend the tone. Using H, 2B, and 4B pencils and a sequence of light and dark scribbles, I create the textures of the bark.

▲ **Step Seven** To finish, I emphasize all the darks with a 4B and lift out highlights where needed. I take a step back and view the drawing from a distance—when I'm pleased with the dark values and light patches of fur, I sign my drawing.

Kitten & Butterfly

▶ **Step One** I start by tracing the outline of the kitten, including the facial features. This kitten is looking up at a butterfly, which I'll add in step 6. I freehand the markings on the kitten's body, and then I transfer the outlines to drawing paper.

▶ **Step Two** I outline the kitten's eyes with a 4B and fill in the pupils, leaving a highlight in each. Then I use a 2B for the iris and blend the tone with a tortillon to achieve a smooth, glassy look. I fill in the nose with a 2B and circular strokes, and I darken the nostril with a 4B. Then I use the 2B to start defining the dark stripes on the head.

▶ **Step Three** With a 4B, I fill in the dark shadows in the ears. I use my kneaded eraser pinched to a sharp edge for the long hair inside the ears. I don't need to draw every hair, as the viewer's eye will fill in what is missing. Next I use a 2H to draw the light hair on the face, avoiding the whiskers. I also darken the stripes on the head. To emphasize the whiskers, I lighten them with my kneaded eraser. Then I begin the stripes on the kitten's body by stroking with a 2B.

▶ **Step Four** Now I darken and refine the dark stripes. I use a sharp 4B with tapering strokes in the direction of hair growth, being careful to leave spaces for individual white hairs. Then I use a 2B for the midtones in the neck area, also leaving spaces for lighter hairs.

▶ **Step Five** Next I use a 2B for the midtones of the kitten's body. I use the same tapering strokes as with the 4B. I occasionally use an H for the lighter hair, such as in the chest area, and a 2B for the longer hair on top of the back. I continue to leave spaces for the lightest hairs. Once all the fur has been laid in, I go back with a 4B and blend the darks with longer, smoother strokes.

▶ **Step Six** I use my kneaded eraser to lift out highlights. Then I go back over the entire kitten with a 4B to accent dark areas for depth. Next I draw the butterfly above the kitten's head. I use a 2B to shade the outer wings, the dark areas of the body, and the antennae. I create the spots by drawing around them (negative drawing), and then I go back with a kneaded eraser to lighten the spots a bit.

▶ **Step Seven** Continuing with the butterfly, I use an H pencil for the lighter areas of the upper wings, a 2H for the center of the lower wings, and a very sharp 4B for the darker areas. Finally, I use a 2B to create the shadow under the kitten, and then I blend the tone with a tortillon for a smooth finish.

Cindy Smith

Fawn

Step One I begin by using tracing paper to create the basic outline of the fawn, including the facial features. After I freehand the identifying markings and map out the values, I transfer the outline to drawing paper.

Step Two I fill in the pupils with a 4B and use a 2B for the outline around the eye, which I blend with a tortillon. Then I fill in the nostrils with a 4B and shade the top of the nose with a 2B, using circular strokes for texture. Next I use my 2B to start defining darker areas on the rest of the fawn.

Step Three I continue to emphasize darker areas of the fawn with a 2B and a fairly light touch, so I can go back later and make any necessary corrections. I work on the ears, using an H pencil and tapering strokes for lighter areas, a 2B for the midtones, and a 4B for the darkest areas. Then I blend the tone with the bristle brush.

Step Four Now I turn my attention to the fawn's head. First I lay in the darker, deeper hairs with a 2B pencil. I use long, tapering strokes and am careful to follow the direction of fur growth.

Step Five For the lighter midtones on the head, I use a 2H pencil and the same long, tapering strokes that I used for the darker tones. Then I work on the foreleg and lighter areas of the body using the same techniques that I did with the head, adding depth with a 4B pencil.

Step Six I begin developing the dark areas on the fawn's back with a 4B, using long, tapering strokes. I leave some areas light for now, as I'll come back to them later. At this point, I concentrate more on following the direction of hair growth than perfecting these dark areas.

◄ **Step Seven** Now I use a 2B pencil to fill in some of the areas on the back that were previously left white. Then I use an H pencil to start creating the background reeds. I fill in the spaces between the reeds with a 4B pencil, spreading the tone with the bristle brush. (You can see the basic outlines for the reeds at the top of this drawing.) Next I use a 2B to add shadows to the reeds that are overlapped by other reeds. I lift out highlights in the overlapping reeds and create the curved edges of the "frame" with my kneaded eraser.

Step Eight I continue shading the reeds and the spaces between the reeds—I want the background to be subtle so it doesn't detract from the fawn, yet I still want it to seem like a natural camouflage for its coat. Finally, I use a 4B to darken all the darks, and I pull out highlights with a kneaded eraser to create more contrast.

Lion Cub

◄ **Step One** I trace the outline of the lion cub, as well as the facial features and the darkest markings of the fur. Then I transfer the drawing to another piece of paper.

► **Step Two** Starting with the eyes, I use a 4B to fill in the pupils and outline the eyes. I shade the darker parts of the iris with a 2B and blend the tone into the lighter areas of the iris with a tortillon. Next I use a 4B for the mouth and nostrils; I use a 2B and circular strokes for the tip of the nose. Then I work from the area below the eyes up to the forehead, establishing the dark, medium, and light tones for the rest of the cub's fur. I lay down the darks first with short, quick, tapering strokes. For the midtones, I use a 2B and longer strokes, occasionally blending with the bristle brush.

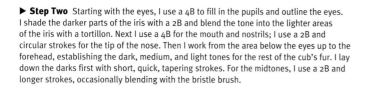

◄ **Step Three** I use a 4B to fill in the dark inner ear, and then I switch to a 2B pencil to begin the midtone tufts of hair on the head. I periodically use the bristle brush to blend and spread the tone. I use my kneaded eraser pinched to a sharp edge and "draw" the lighter hairs, which lifts out the tone I applied with the bristle brush. By looking at the cub's left ear, you can see how I lay in the patterns of the fur before adding the darker areas.

► **Step Four** I work down the bridge of the nose with a dull 4B, laying in the darker areas with short strokes. I also use the 4B for the dark areas at the base of the whiskers and below the mouth. I lay in the midtones with a 2B, establishing the various tones of the fur on either side of the nose.

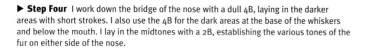

◀ **Step Five** Now I use a very sharp 4B to lay in the dark hairs along the nose. Then I use my 2B to start identifying the dark areas on the paws and chest, carefully drawing around the whiskers to make them stand out.

▶ **Step Six** Now I work on the rest of the cub's body. I use a dull 2B for the midtones, following the direction of fur growth. For the shorter hair on the leg, I use a scribbling motion and then blend with a tortillon. I use a 4B for the darkest darks. Then I lift out highlights and the small hairs on the paws with a kneaded eraser.

Step Seven I emphasize the darks and lights all over the cub for greater contrast. Then I create a light cast shadow with a 2B pencil, lightly blending the tone with a tortillon. For darker shadows, I add another layer of tone in the same manner. Now my drawing is complete!

YORKIE PUPPY

Step One I trace the major outlines of this adorable Yorkie puppy and the teacup using tracing paper. Then I freehand the whiskers and fur markings of the dog and transfer the drawing to another piece of paper.

Step Two I begin shading by outlining the eyes and lightly filling in the irises with a 4B pencil, blending the tone in the irises with a tortillon. I also fill in the pupils, using heavier pressure and leaving a highlight in each. I shade the nose with circular strokes and a 4B pencil, and I create the dark area under the nose with a 2B. I start establishing the darker areas of the head with a 4B, creating some midtones by blending the tone with the bristle brush. Then I use a 2B and long, tapering strokes for the midtones of the ears; I blend the tone inside the ears with a tortillon to make it look like skin.

Step Three I continue working on the head, alternating between an H and a 2B for the lighter and midtone areas, respectively. I use long, tapering strokes, being careful to follow the direction of the hair. I periodically "draw" lighter hairs by lifting out tone with my kneaded eraser pinched to a sharp edge, and I use a 4B to add a few darker hairs throughout for depth. I also draw darker individual hairs over the lighter hairs in various directions for a more natural appearance. Then I start on the whiskers at the sides of the nose with an H pencil.

Step Four Next I use a 4B to darken the darks, bringing out the highlighted hair. I continue lifting out lighter hairs with my pinched eraser, and I periodically blend and spread the tone with the bristle brush. I start laying in the darker areas of the paws with a 2B, leaving white areas for the lighter hairs. I switch to working on the teacup before finishing the paws so I can make the paws overlap the teacup. I use an H pencil to cover the entire cup with long, even strokes that are close together. I add another layer of H pencil for the darker areas of the cup and saucer. I continue defining the darks of the teacup and saucer with a sharp 2B pencil. I use a 4B for the outline and stems of the flowers and a 2B for the darkest flowers. Then I use a 2B to add dark shading to the outer edges of the cup and saucer, achieving a rounded look. Next I create the darks of the paws with a 4B pencil.

▶ Step Five I finish the paws by adding midtones with a 2B pencil. Finally, I go over the whole drawing, darkening the darks with a 4B and lifting out highlights with my kneaded eraser to increase the contrast of the drawing.

LAMB

▶ **Step One** I begin by using tracing paper to create the outline of the lamb's body and facial features. Then I freehand the light and dark areas of the wool, using loose, bumpy lines rather than hard, straight lines. I also freehand the blades of grass. Now I transfer the outlines to drawing paper.

▶ **Step Two** I use a 4B to create the darkest areas of the eyes, nose, and mouth. Then I blend the eyes with a tortillon. I create small, circular strokes to create texture on the nose, using a 4B for the darker areas and a 2H for the lighter areas.

▶ **Step Three** I use a dull 4B with soft, loose, circular strokes to begin establishing the darks and shadowed areas of the wool. I use closer, tighter, circular strokes for the darker areas of wool and loose, light strokes for the lighter areas. Then I blend and soften my strokes with a tortillon.

▶ **Step Four** I continue working on the wool with 2B and 4B pencils. I blend the tone over the forms of the body (such as the belly and chest) with a tortillon, and then I use the bristle brush to spread light tone all over the wool. Then I create deeper areas in the wool with a 2B.

▲ Step Five I use my kneaded eraser to lift out highlights in the wool. Then I go back with my 4B pencil to reinforce the dark areas of the eyes, nose, and mouth. I use a 2B to emphasize the dark areas of the wool. Then I begin the grass by sketching the blades with a 2H pencil.

▶ Step Six I use a 2B to fill in the spaces between the blades of grass; then I add tone to the blades with the bristle brush and reinforce the shadows with a 2B pencil. As a final touch, I lift out highlights on some of the blades using a kneaded eraser.

Cindy Smith

GIRAFFE CALF

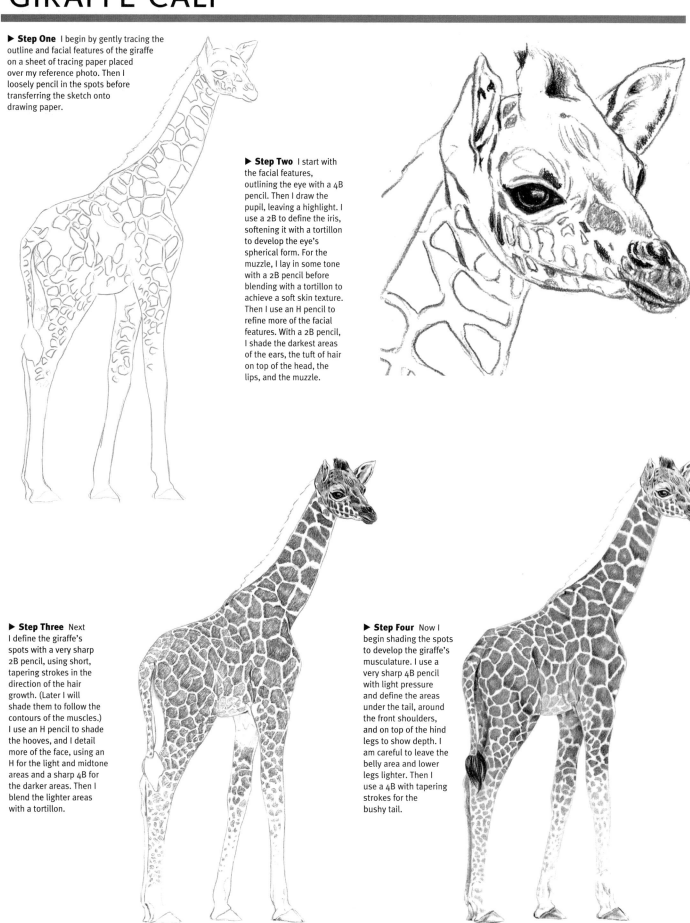

▶ **Step One** I begin by gently tracing the outline and facial features of the giraffe on a sheet of tracing paper placed over my reference photo. Then I loosely pencil in the spots before transferring the sketch onto drawing paper.

▶ **Step Two** I start with the facial features, outlining the eye with a 4B pencil. Then I draw the pupil, leaving a highlight. I use a 2B to define the iris, softening it with a tortillon to develop the eye's spherical form. For the muzzle, I lay in some tone with a 2B pencil before blending with a tortillon to achieve a soft skin texture. Then I use an H pencil to refine more of the facial features. With a 2B pencil, I shade the darkest areas of the ears, the tuft of hair on top of the head, the lips, and the muzzle.

▶ **Step Three** Next I define the giraffe's spots with a very sharp 2B pencil, using short, tapering strokes in the direction of the hair growth. (Later I will shade them to follow the contours of the muscles.) I use an H pencil to shade the hooves, and I detail more of the face, using an H for the light and midtone areas and a sharp 4B for the darker areas. Then I blend the lighter areas with a tortillon.

▶ **Step Four** Now I begin shading the spots to develop the giraffe's musculature. I use a very sharp 4B pencil with light pressure and define the areas under the tail, around the front shoulders, and on top of the hind legs to show depth. I am careful to leave the belly area and lower legs lighter. Then I use a 4B with tapering strokes for the bushy tail.

▶ **Step Five** Next I start on the mane. I use a 2B for the lighter area at the base and switch to a 4B for the darker middle area, then back to a 2B with gentle pressure for the lighter ends. Using the bristle brush, I blend the mane with a sweeping motion in the direction of the hair growth. As this may add tone around the mane, I use my kneaded eraser to clean up any areas that should remain white.

◀ **Step Six** Now I go over the entire giraffe, emphasizing the darkest areas with a 4B and lightening the brightest areas with a kneaded eraser for contrast. I add a suggestion of grass to ground the calf. I use an H pencil to draw the blades and a 4B to darken the spaces between them. Then I add tone to the grass using a 2B and blend it with the bristle brush. I use my kneaded eraser pinched to a sharp edge to create a few lighter blades for depth and dimension.

About the Artist

Cindy Smith has been interested in art all of her life—she's been winning awards for her drawings ever since grade school. Most recently, she won first place in several art competitions and a people's choice award at local art shows. While for years she painted with oil and acrylic paints, she now focuses on fine pencil work. It is not unusual for Cindy to spend 40 to 100 hours on a single drawing! Cindy creates depth and movement with the use of perspective, rich tonality, and a number of rendering techniques that bring her drawings to life. When she's not at her "real job," she renders commissions throughout the United States and Canada, depicting everything from portraits and pets to buildings and boats.

Following her travels, Cindy returned to her native state of Idaho. Surrounded by both mountains and desert, she made her home in Boise because she enjoys the diverse terrain she grew up with. Cindy is married with two children.